Shopping List

Meal Planner

	Lunch	Evening Meal
Monday		
Tuesday		
Wednesday		
Thursday		
Friday		
Saturday		
Sunday		
Notes		

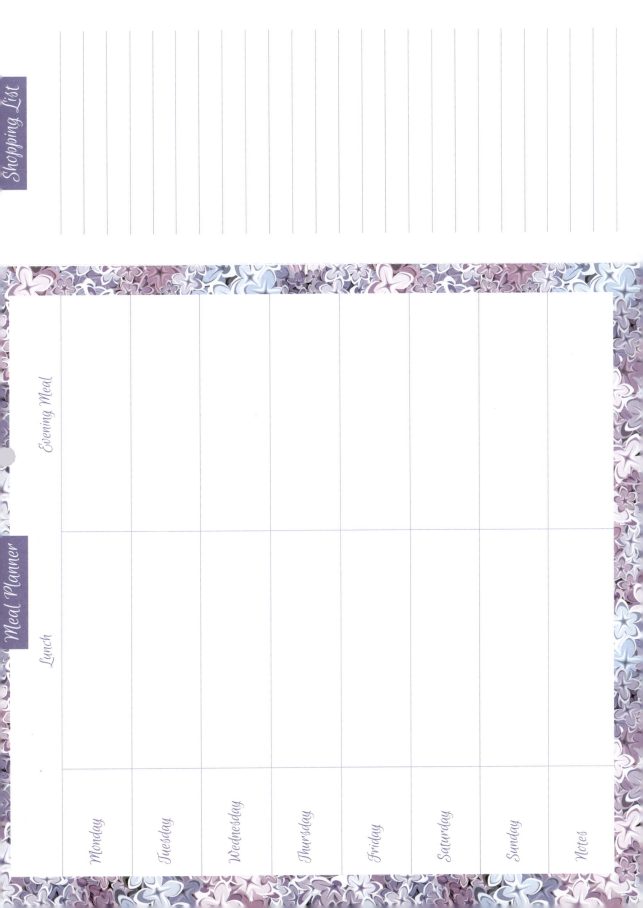

Shopping List

Meal Planner

	Lunch	Evening Meal
Monday		
Tuesday		
Wednesday		
Thursday		
Friday		
Saturday		
Sunday		
Notes		

Shopping List

Meal Planner

	Lunch	Evening Meal
Monday		
Tuesday		
Wednesday		
Thursday		
Friday		
Saturday		
Sunday		
Notes		

Shopping List

Meal Planner

	Lunch	Evening Meal
Monday		
Tuesday		
Wednesday		
Thursday		
Friday		
Saturday		
Sunday		
Notes		

Shopping List

Meal Planner

	Lunch	Evening Meal
Monday		
Tuesday		
Wednesday		
Thursday		
Friday		
Saturday		
Sunday		
Notes		

Shopping List

Meal Planner

	Lunch	Evening Meal
Monday		
Tuesday		
Wednesday		
Thursday		
Friday		
Saturday		
Sunday		
Notes		

Shopping List

Meal Planner

	Lunch	Evening Meal
Monday		
Tuesday		
Wednesday		
Thursday		
Friday		
Saturday		
Sunday		
Notes		

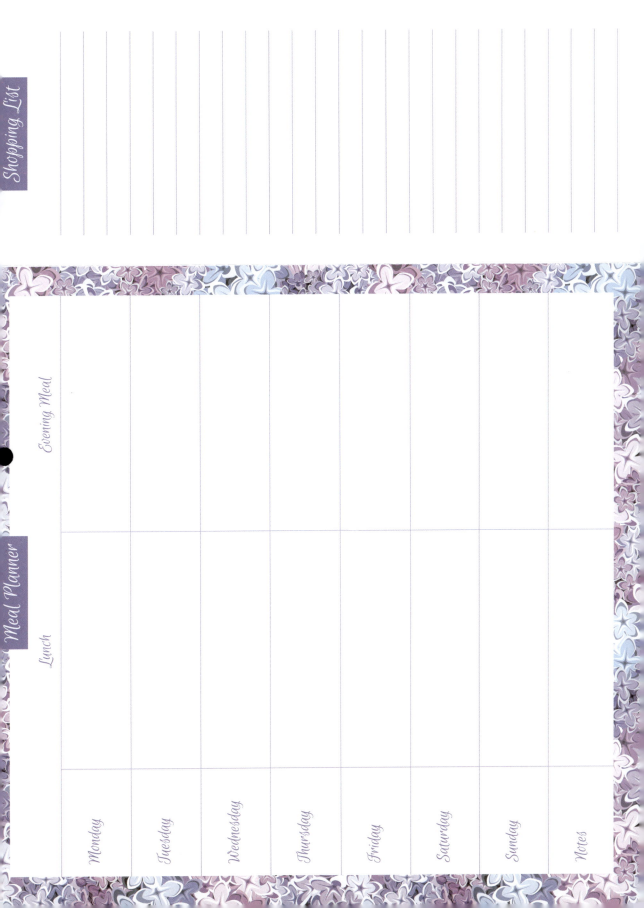

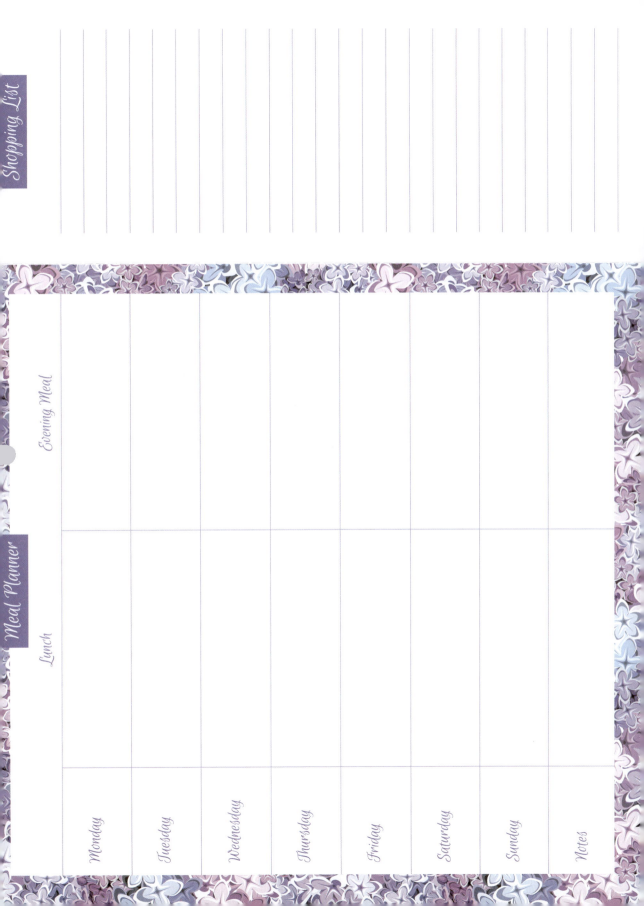

Shopping List

Meal Planner

	Lunch	Evening Meal
Monday		
Tuesday		
Wednesday		
Thursday		
Friday		
Saturday		
Sunday		
Notes		

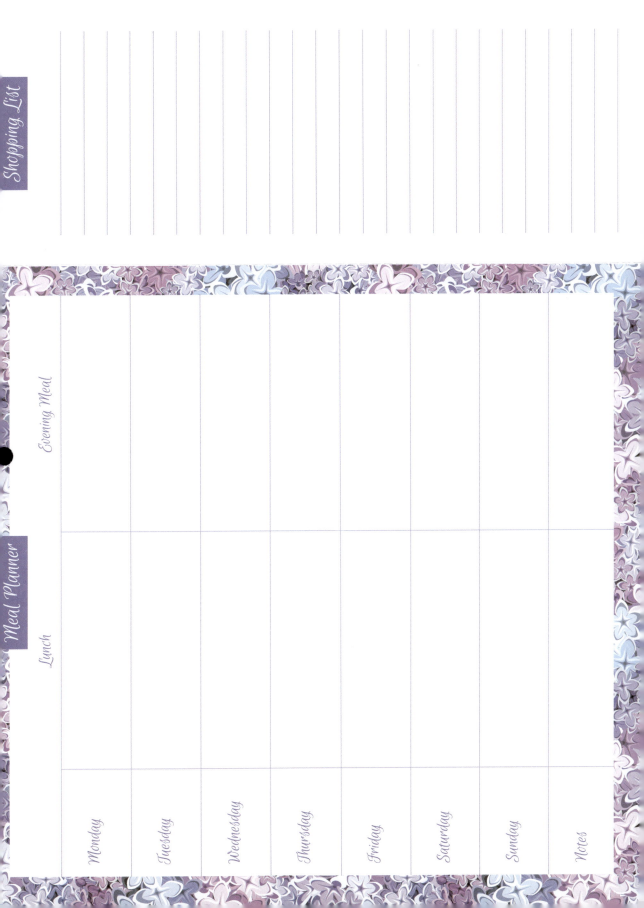

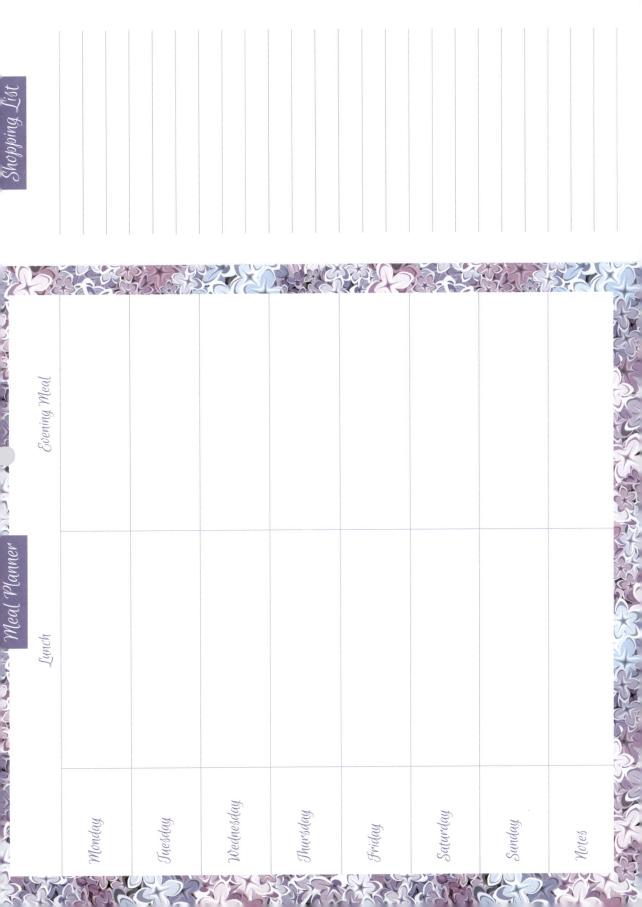

Shopping List

Meal Planner

	Lunch	Evening Meal
Monday		
Tuesday		
Wednesday		
Thursday		
Friday		
Saturday		
Sunday		
Notes		

Shopping List

Meal Planner

	Lunch	Evening Meal
Monday		
Tuesday		
Wednesday		
Thursday		
Friday		
Saturday		
Sunday		
Notes		

Shopping List

Meal Planner

	Lunch	Evening Meal
Monday		
Tuesday		
Wednesday		
Thursday		
Friday		
Saturday		
Sunday		
Notes		

Shopping List

Meal Planner

	Evening Meal		Lunch
Monday			
Tuesday			
Wednesday			
Thursday			
Friday			
Saturday			
Sunday			
Notes			

Shopping List

Meal Planner

	Lunch	Evening Meal
Monday		
Tuesday		
Wednesday		
Thursday		
Friday		
Saturday		
Sunday		
Notes		

Shopping List

Meal Planner

	Lunch	Evening Meal
Monday		
Tuesday		
Wednesday		
Thursday		
Friday		
Saturday		
Sunday		
Notes		

Shopping List

Meal Planner

	Lunch	Evening Meal
Monday		
Tuesday		
Wednesday		
Thursday		
Friday		
Saturday		
Sunday		
Notes		

Shopping List

Meal Planner

	Lunch	Evening Meal
Monday		
Tuesday		
Wednesday		
Thursday		
Friday		
Saturday		
Sunday		
Notes		

Shopping List

Meal Planner

	Lunch	Evening Meal
Monday		
Tuesday		
Wednesday		
Thursday		
Friday		
Saturday		
Sunday		
Notes		

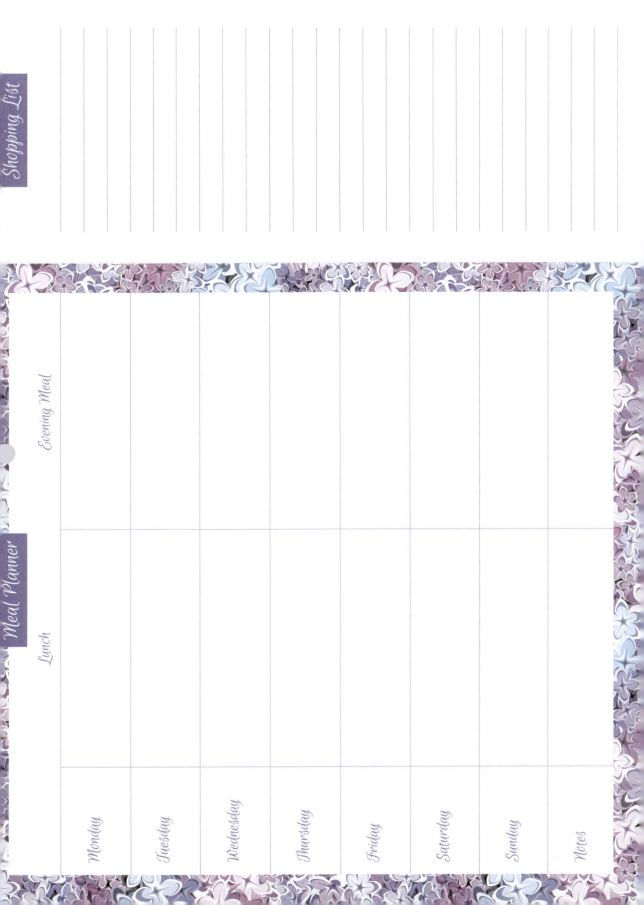

Shopping List

Meal Planner

	Lunch	Evening Meal
Monday		
Tuesday		
Wednesday		
Thursday		
Friday		
Saturday		
Sunday		
Notes		

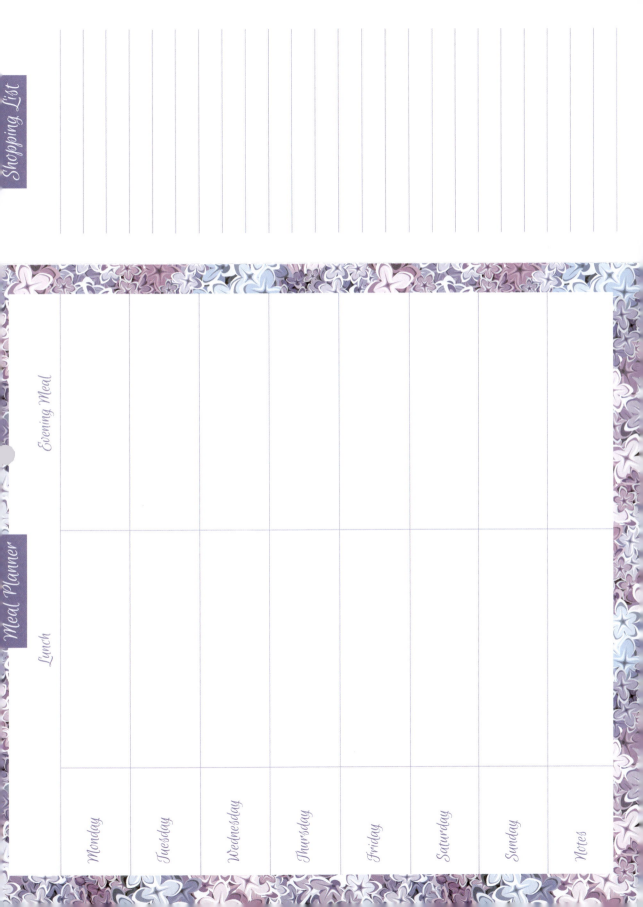

Shopping List

Meal Planner

Evening Meal

Lunch

Monday

Tuesday

Wednesday

Thursday

Friday

Saturday

Sunday

Notes

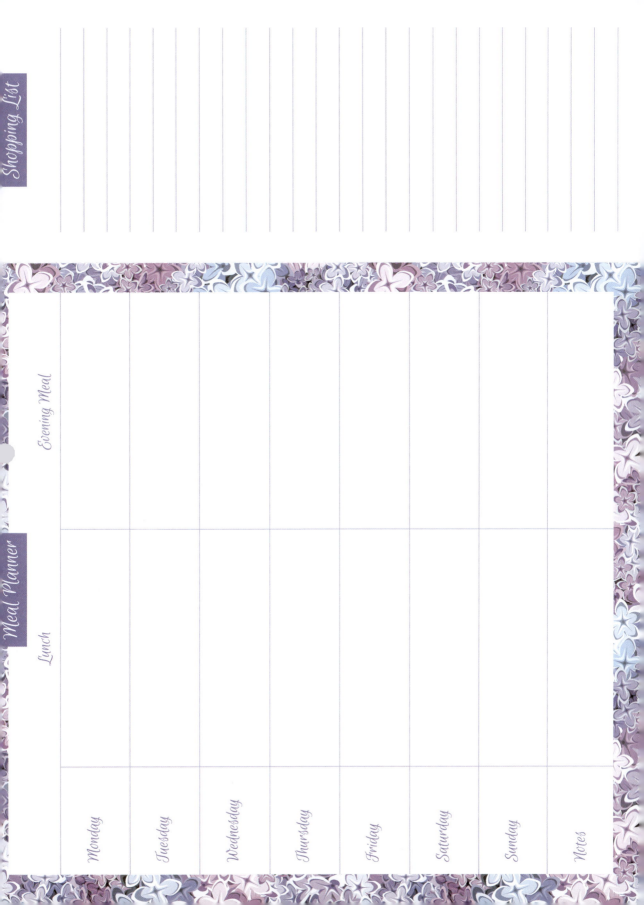

Shopping List

Meal Planner

	Evening Meal				Lunch		
Monday							
Tuesday							
Wednesday							
Thursday							
Friday							
Saturday							
Sunday							
Notes							

Shopping List

Meal Planner

	Lunch	Evening Meal
Monday		
Tuesday		
Wednesday		
Thursday		
Friday		
Saturday		
Sunday		
Notes		

Shopping List

Meal Planner

	Evening Meal		Lunch	
Monday				
Tuesday				
Wednesday				
Thursday				
Friday				
Saturday				
Sunday				
Notes				

Shopping List

Meal Planner

	Lunch	Evening Meal
Monday		
Tuesday		
Wednesday		
Thursday		
Friday		
Saturday		
Sunday		
Notes		

Shopping List

Meal Planner

	Lunch	Evening Meal
Monday		
Tuesday		
Wednesday		
Thursday		
Friday		
Saturday		
Sunday		
Notes		

Shopping List

Meal Planner

	Lunch	Evening Meal
Monday		
Tuesday		
Wednesday		
Thursday		
Friday		
Saturday		
Sunday		
Notes		

Shopping List

Meal Planner

	Lunch		Evening Meal	
Monday				
Tuesday				
Wednesday				
Thursday				
Friday				
Saturday				
Sunday				
Notes				

Shopping List

Meal Planner

	Lunch	Evening Meal
Monday		
Tuesday		
Wednesday		
Thursday		
Friday		
Saturday		
Sunday		
Notes		

Shopping List

Meal Planner

	Lunch	Evening Meal
Monday		
Tuesday		
Wednesday		
Thursday		
Friday		
Saturday		
Sunday		
Notes		

Shopping List

Meal Planner

	Lunch	Evening Meal
Monday		
Tuesday		
Wednesday		
Thursday		
Friday		
Saturday		
Sunday		
Notes		

Shopping List

Meal Planner

	Evening Meal	Lunch
Monday		
Tuesday		
Wednesday		
Thursday		
Friday		
Saturday		
Sunday		
Notes		

Shopping List

Meal Planner

	Lunch	Evening Meal
Monday		
Tuesday		
Wednesday		
Thursday		
Friday		
Saturday		
Sunday		
Notes		

Shopping List

Meal Planner

	Lunch	Evening Meal
Monday		
Tuesday		
Wednesday		
Thursday		
Friday		
Saturday		
Sunday		
Notes		

Shopping List

Meal Planner

	Lunch	Evening Meal
Monday		
Tuesday		
Wednesday		
Thursday		
Friday		
Saturday		
Sunday		
Notes		

Shopping List

Meal Planner

	Lunch	Evening Meal
Monday		
Tuesday		
Wednesday		
Thursday		
Friday		
Saturday		
Sunday		
Notes		

Shopping List

Meal Planner

	Lunch	Evening Meal
Monday		
Tuesday		
Wednesday		
Thursday		
Friday		
Saturday		
Sunday		
Notes		

Shopping List

Meal Planner

	Lunch	Evening Meal
Monday		
Tuesday		
Wednesday		
Thursday		
Friday		
Saturday		
Sunday		
Notes		

Shopping List

Meal Planner

	Lunch	Evening Meal
Monday		
Tuesday		
Wednesday		
Thursday		
Friday		
Saturday		
Sunday		
Notes		

Shopping List

Meal Planner

	Lunch	Evening Meal
Monday		
Tuesday		
Wednesday		
Thursday		
Friday		
Saturday		
Sunday		
Notes		

Shopping List

Meal Planner

	Lunch	Evening Meal
Monday		
Tuesday		
Wednesday		
Thursday		
Friday		
Saturday		
Sunday		
Notes		

Shopping List

Meal Planner

	Lunch	Evening Meal
Monday		
Tuesday		
Wednesday		
Thursday		
Friday		
Saturday		
Sunday		
Notes		

Shopping List

Meal Planner

	Lunch	Evening Meal
Monday		
Tuesday		
Wednesday		
Thursday		
Friday		
Saturday		
Sunday		
Notes		

Shopping List

Meal Planner

	Lunch	Evening Meal
Monday		
Tuesday		
Wednesday		
Thursday		
Friday		
Saturday		
Sunday		
Notes		

Shopping List

Meal Planner

	Lunch	Evening Meal
Monday		
Tuesday		
Wednesday		
Thursday		
Friday		
Saturday		
Sunday		
Notes		

Shopping List

Meal Planner

	Lunch	Evening Meal
Monday		
Tuesday		
Wednesday		
Thursday		
Friday		
Saturday		
Sunday		
Notes		

Shopping List

Meal Planner

	Lunch	Evening Meal
Monday		
Tuesday		
Wednesday		
Thursday		
Friday		
Saturday		
Sunday		
Notes		

Shopping List

Meal Planner

	Lunch	Evening Meal
Monday		
Tuesday		
Wednesday		
Thursday		
Friday		
Saturday		
Sunday		
Notes		

Shopping List

Meal Planner

	Lunch	Evening Meal
Monday		
Tuesday		
Wednesday		
Thursday		
Friday		
Saturday		
Sunday		
Notes		

Shopping List

Meal Planner

	Lunch	Evening Meal
Monday		
Tuesday		
Wednesday		
Thursday		
Friday		
Saturday		
Sunday		
Notes		

Shopping List

Meal Planner

	Lunch	Evening Meal
Monday		
Tuesday		
Wednesday		
Thursday		
Friday		
Saturday		
Sunday		
Notes		

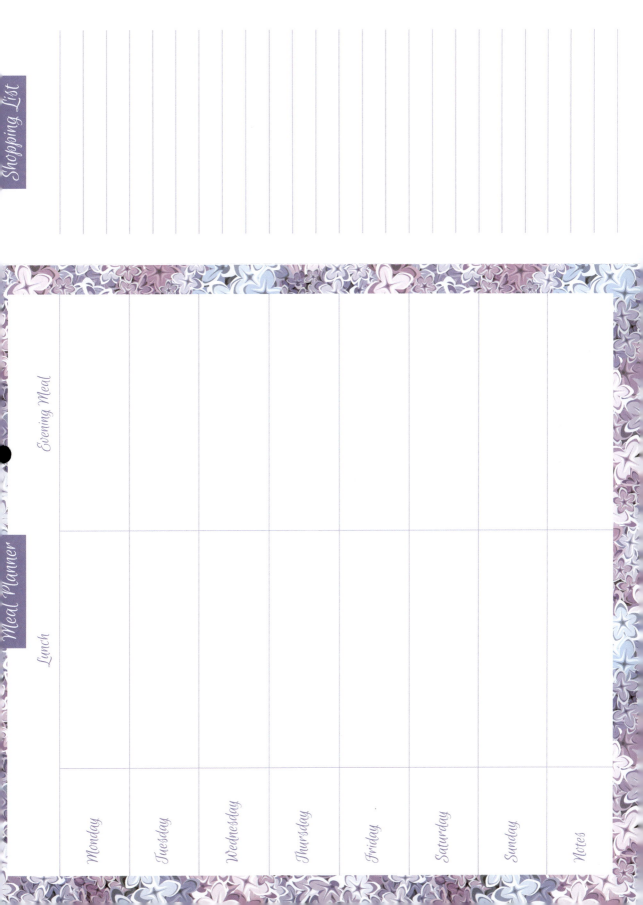

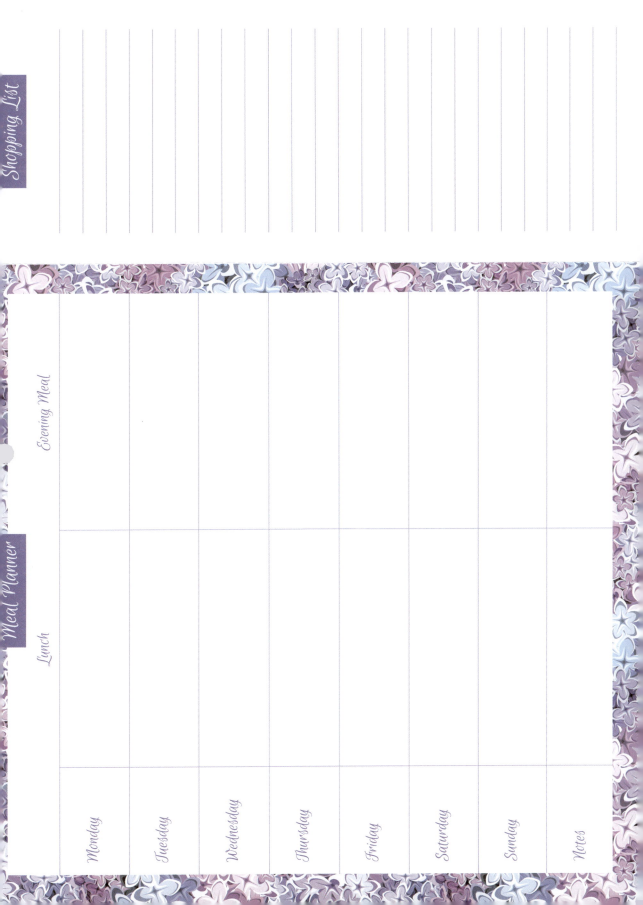

Shopping List

Meal Planner

	Lunch	Evening Meal
Monday		
Tuesday		
Wednesday		
Thursday		
Friday		
Saturday		
Sunday		
Notes		

Shopping List

Meal Planner

	Lunch	Evening Meal
Monday		
Tuesday		
Wednesday		
Thursday		
Friday		
Saturday		
Sunday		
Notes		

Shopping List

Meal Planner

	Lunch	Evening Meal
Monday		
Tuesday		
Wednesday		
Thursday		
Friday		
Saturday		
Sunday		
Notes		

Shopping List

Meal Planner

	Lunch	Evening Meal
Monday		
Tuesday		
Wednesday		
Thursday		
Friday		
Saturday		
Sunday		
Notes		

Shopping List

Meal Planner

	Lunch	Evening Meal
Monday		
Tuesday		
Wednesday		
Thursday		
Friday		
Saturday		
Sunday		
Notes		

Shopping List

Meal Planner

	Lunch	Evening Meal
Monday		
Tuesday		
Wednesday		
Thursday		
Friday		
Saturday		
Sunday		
Notes		

Shopping List

Meal Planner

	Lunch			Evening Meal		
Monday						
Tuesday						
Wednesday						
Thursday						
Friday						
Saturday						
Sunday						
Notes						

Shopping List

Meal Planner

	Lunch	Evening Meal
Monday		
Tuesday		
Wednesday		
Thursday		
Friday		
Saturday		
Sunday		
Notes		

Shopping List

Meal Planner

	Lunch	Evening Meal
Monday		
Tuesday		
Wednesday		
Thursday		
Friday		
Saturday		
Sunday		
Notes		

Shopping List

Meal Planner

	Lunch	Evening Meal
Monday		
Tuesday		
Wednesday		
Thursday		
Friday		
Saturday		
Sunday		
Notes		